Apricot
Toast

Apricot
Toast

THREE
GENERATIONS
OF POETS

THE CHOIR PRESS

First published in the United Kingdom in 2021 by
The Choir Press

ISBN 978-1-78963-205-7

My Dad, Peter Cross, would have been 100 in 2020 (had he lived a very few more years) and to honour that and the inspiration he gave us, this anthology celebrates his poetry, my own and those of my twins, Subira and Wandia. Inevitably, our styles are very different, although along with his more formal poems, Dad wrote several funny or nonsense poems for the twins when they were little. Subira and Wandia are known as performance poets, but a few of their poems work on the page too and some are represented here.

We hope you enjoy what we offer, as much as we love creating poems.

Merry

Dedication

This anthology is dedicated to the memory of both my father Peter, some of whose poems feature here, and my mother Doris. I loved them both deeply.

I have written more about Dad later, but Mum loved literature and taught me so much about words. What's more it was she who patiently typed out all my Dad's poems.

Acknowledgements

Thanks are due to Ron Roberts who so often encouraged me to try to get my work published. Also I need to thank staff at The Choir Press for patiently answering my rookie questions!

It has been wonderful too having the support and insights of Wandia and Subira throughout.

Contents

LOVE   1

A Word Across the Seas	Peter	2
My Valentine	Peter	3
Love's Melody	Peter	4
Moira	Peter	5
For Teri: It's Terminal, but …	Merry	6
For Teri: In Her Last Weeks	Merry	7
Molasses of Care	Wandia	8

EAST AFRICA   11

A Poem at Dawn	Merry	12
In a Former Life	Merry	14
Duluti	Peter	15
Fling Wide the Window of Morning	Merry	16
To An African Child	Merry	18
Dayenu	Merry	19

PLAYFULNESS   21

Apricot Toast	Peter	22
Suarez Soaking	Merry	23
Take Two	Merry	24
Poor Potomous	Peter	25
For Emusement	Peter	26
Oh, Twins!	Subira & Wandia	27
Uh Oh	Merry	30

SNAPSHOTS   31

Just an Ordinary Day   Peter   32
Pipe Smoke   Peter   33
Images From An Autumn Garden   Merry   34
Night Light   Merry   35
Acupuncture Treatment   Merry   36
Sculpture Trail   Merry   37
In a Pandemic ... At Least   Merry   38

MESSAGES   39

To Thine Own Self Be True   Peter   40
On Your 14th Birthday, Maya   Merry   41
I Can   Peter   42
No Hurry   Peter   43
For Dad at 75   Merry   44
I Will Be Happy to Leave
  (This Earth To You)   Merry   45
Comfort Your Hearts Dear Friends Merry   46
Don't Touch My Hair   Wandia   48

RAGE AND RESISTANCE   51

My Background   Wandia   52
We Should Have Seen it Coming   Merry   54
Care   Merry   56
Villanelle: This Vast Entitled
  Bag of Air   Merry   57
Cuddly Cummings   Merry   58
I'm Trying (But so are the times) Merry   60
Coffee and Cream   Subira   61
Reverse Racism and
Other White Tears   Subira   64
Clearing Out the Trash   Subira   67
Where Are You From?   Subira & Wandia   70

Dad was born into quite a wealthy family and was therefore sent to a public school, which he absolutely loathed! He was bullied, because he was small and Jewish and perhaps this made him introspective. His older brother Teddy was killed fighting the fascists in the Spanish Civil War and one of Dad's relatives wrote a very moving poem in tribute to Teddy. Maybe this also inspired Dad to create poems.

My parents met at a social group organised by the local synagogue and they rapidly realised they both loved theatre and trying their hands at acting. So they were already very much in love when the Second World War came along. Dad enlisted in the Royal Air Force and became a pilot. But he was never one to glory in any aspect of the war, barely ever speaking about it. Yet one of the things he eventually told me was that while most of his colleagues spent free evenings drinking together, Dad would retire to his bunk and write love poems. In this selection, you will find poems written before and during the war.

After the war, he got a job in marketing with what was then the United Africa Company and after a spell in Nigeria, was sent to Kenya where he was joined by my mother and sister. I was born there and eventually we all moved to what is now Tanzania. This is where Dad gazed at Lake Duluti and wrote the poem you will find here.

He carried on writing throughout his life (though much more spasmodically inevitably) and you will find one dedicated to the memory of Moira who was at one time a much loved neighbour of ours. She died prematurely of cancer and was much missed. Indeed Dad stayed in touch with Moira's husband and children until the end of his life.

MERRY

Although I was born in Kenya, we all came back here when I was an infant, because I had a bafflingly rare physical impairment. However, in my thirties I was overwhelmed by the need to return to my birthplace to understand what it really meant to me. You will discover that for yourselves in the Kenya poems. My twins are of mixed heritage – white British and black African.

My identity as a disabled woman emerges strongly in some of these poems, particularly those I have written more recently.

The pandemic has drawn many poems from me, the latest being for children, which you will hopefully see more of at a later date!

Villanelle: This Vast Entitled Bag of Air was first published in Coronaverses, Roundhead, April 2020

SUBIRA AND WANDIA

My twins were born here in England, but Wandia now lives in Germany, whilst Subira remains here. Their reputations as performance poets separately and together, keep growing.

SUBIRA

Subira Joy is a queer, Black, non-binary spoken word poet and activist. Their pronouns are they/them/theirs. Creator of award winning solo spoken word show "Subira" and co-creator of "Joy Nduku" with twin Wandia, their work weaves together the personal and political, through experiences and imaginations, spoken with rage, softness, and laughter.

More recently, Subira has been stepping into the realm of live art and performance, and hopes to continue in a journey of expression and experimentation.

WANDIA NDUKU

Wandia Nduku (they/them) is a spoken word artist from the UK living in Hamburg, Germany. They are an unapologetically Black queer migrant, who strives to find power in voicing vulnerability. Anger, pain and frustration meet love, hope and pleasure in their poetry. Since 2015, Wandia has been performing spoken word, appearing on stages in the UK, Germany and Finland. Wandia is co-creator of 'Joy Nduku', a spoken word show they devised and performed with their twin, and is currently exploring the incorporation of musical and rhythmical elements into their poetry.

Love

A Word Across the Seas

Be not unhappy now I am abroad.
Seems it you far that I have gone away?
Seems the sea deep? A stream you cannot ford?
Seems it you I have night whilst you have day?

Listen my love, a word in your ear.
Let me replace the laughter in your eye,
Gladden your heart and smile away that tear.
Lift up your heart. Your answer in the sky.

Look at the stars. Between, a deeper space
Than any lengths of land or depths of sea.
In the unknown for years the comets pass.
Seems not the distance small from you to me?

Water that laps on my shore laps on thine.
Sun that I see is seen by you each day.
Lift up your eyes and in the sky see mine.
Happy your heart, mine own, when I'm away.

PETER

My Valentine

I'll love you thro' the days and thro' the years,
And evergreen my love, as mountain pine.
I beg to share your laughter and your tears
My Valentine.

I wish to share your cup, our lips as one,
Together drinking deeply of life's wine
From which the web of happiness is spun,
My Valentine.

We'll walk together in a woodland glade,
And watch autumnal leaves the dry grass line,
But memory born of love can never fade
My Valentine.

This poem is but little of my love,
A glimmer of that golden thread divine,
Alive in me. You are my very heart,
My Valentine.

PETER

Love's Melody

The love we hear is like a melody,
Upon my heart is played, on yours is heard;
Our eyes go through, divine the other's thoughts,
And tell of peace and joy – yet speak no word.
And thus together with our hearts in tune,
Which gently pulse into a steady beat,
We live, love, breathe as one, our souls combine,
And in those hours our happiness complete.

PETER

Moira

In our garden Moira's living
With her fragrance everywhere,
Perfumes sweet of selfless giving
Colouring the fertile air.
Ours the earth in which she planted
Seeds which we must see still thrive.
Ours the privilege she granted,
We to see she stays alive.

PETER

For Teri: It's Terminal, but . . .

Be outrageous to the end,
My friend.
So many rules for you to bend
And bigots to offend
You can set an online trend!
Be outrageous to the end.

Be outrageous just for fun,
Then cut and run!
Tear up copies of The Sun
Chuck a large currant bun.
Bet you'll never be outdone.
Be outrageous, just for fun.

MERRY

For Teri: In Her Last Weeks

Dearest friend
You brought so much to my life
Always listening and learning
To ease my working days
Always warm and friendly
To my whole wayward family
Easing our passage thru'
Terrible teenage years!
Always ready to giggle with me
As we poked fun at pompousness
Easing us thru' dry days
In front of the computer
Always supportive of me
Easing my path thru'
Physical and emotional traumas.

I am more grateful to you
Than you can ever know
And I love you deeply....
Or as the twins and I said,
Very, very, very, very, very, very MUCH!!!

MERRY

Molasses of Care

We got timeless spaces
Spaces where time stands still
Spaces where love feels thick in the air, molasses of care
Stretching thousands of miles through underground
cables
Effortlessly

We got timeless spaces
Spaces where distance shrinks
Spaces where kilometers are just pixel small and my
heart feels so full
Sharing moments across time-zones
So easily

I mean, I got up an hour ago and they're about to go to
sleep, and I know a lack of routine has not exactly been
great for my sleeping rhythm, but today? Today, I had a
reason to get out of bed so I'm dressed before dark for
once

And in these spaces I'm staying up abnormally late to
play a cardless card game with familiar strangers, I'm
waking up at an absurd time to take part in a workshop
with loved ones I haven't even met yet

And I'm watching someone cradling a cup of coffee in
their pajamas whilst a late afternoon sun makes my
camera quality even worse than it normally is

We got timeless spaces
Spaces where time stands still
Spaces where love feels thick in the air, molasses of care
Stretching thousands of miles through underground
cables
Effortlessly

We got timeless spaces
Spaces where we can be our best selves
Spaces where bubbles of laughter erupt, isolation
interrupted
Even if it's just
Momentarily

And someone's tumbling out of a bus and into a train
and someone else is walking down a dusty red road and
I breathe in the smells of their far away lives
interspersed into the incense burning by my window

Where I swear I can feel warmth emitting from my
keyboard, and it's not like overheating, it's like the sun
shining in your window has made it over to me

And I know it's not easy
I know you feel isolated
We're together in that
I know people who never felt so alone
People who lost thei'r will to live dropped like keys down a
gutter
Feels like nothing even matters anymore
And these are not isolated incidents, they're insidious in
their incidence
And it only its make it more important that we never
stop

Making timeless spaces
Spaces where time stands still
Spaces where love feels thick in the air, molasses of care
Stretching thousands of miles through underground
cables
Effortlessly

WANDIA

East Africa

A Poem at Dawn

To wake to a deep dark sky fairly bursting with stars
and watch one wink at the moon before diving joyful
into the vastness, its spirit flashing briefly in its wake

To stand all smiles and wonder, almost falling, first for
lack of any anchor save a reeling gravity and then
because a kitten's winding, purring, round my legs

To eat a warming breakfast watching all the while a soft
rose glowing growing `gainst the lines of hills and trees
they showing off their silhouetted beauty as the rosy
    peach
burgeons into warmest orange `neath a pale pale sky

To weep sweet grateful tears, my heart awash with
    beauty,
agog with excitement at the birth-of-the-day party for
a tingling new African Highlands and Rift Valley child

To know I must walk in it; so seeing the sparkle of a soft
night's dewdrops on blades of grass and rich green
leaves,
hearing the crickets (seemingly gathered for a concert
round one tree)

all having a final fling before an invisible conductor
waves them silent, so the small birds can, laughing
      almost,
sing and celebrate and vainly try to drown
the cock-a-doodle-doos bouncing madly round the
      valley

To gaze lovingly at gentle thatched mud huts
which stir and mumble, people stumbling from their
      sleep,
splashing cold cold water – then warming over fires
that send their fragrant haze of smoke to drift up lightly
through those yielding rooves

To see the sun itself peeking cheekily brilliant under
it's now lemon and silver blue canopy and watch the
      very
first shafts bounce with glorious brightness on the fields
and-all-in-the-same-moment the day's first shadows fall
mine included.

To be a part of this seems all I ever wanted
and I wanted
to share it with you.

                                                    MERRY

13

In a Former Life

I must have been a lizard
In a former life.
I still love to be still
Dressed in bright colours
The sun on my back
Soaking warmth
Into my skin
Into my blood
Into my very being.

MERRY

Duluti

When mountains sprang in angry birth
And sky reflected flame,
Out of the passion of the earth
Quiet Lake Duluti came.

The hollow of Mount Meru's hand
Cradles the crater lake;
Whilst clear rejuvenating springs
Will man's tired flesh rewake.

Duluti – when the sun is hot –
To feel your cool embrace!
The liquid velvet round one's limbs,
The ripples at one's face.

With Nature's brush the colours laid
With Nature's pencil lined,
Engraved in wonder is the lake,
Forever in one's mind.

PETER

15

Fling Wide the Window of Morning

Fling wide the window of morning
and let the dawn's fragrant hope
fill your spirit.
> For the day is fresh
> and new to the mould of your own creating.

Give the growing hours your love
and earth and sky will meet
in your embrace.
> For Love is the living thread
> weaving your very soul into life's fabric.

Then, in the night's dreaming
seek to solve your problems
with beauty.
> For dreams tap the gold
> of your spirit and may bring you singing
> to the next new day.

Or HOW IT REALLY WAS.
Fling wide the window of morning
and let the fragrant smoke
of someone else's jiko* choke
your passages.

Pull back the curtains of dawning
and duck the mbu's[†] dive
and, dancing, strive
to keep from being bitten.

Put your head into the morning air
and observe the cloud dark skies
with your sleep befuddled eyes –

then creep back into bed and hide.
Let others start the new day
it's safer that way.

MERRY

---

* 'jiko' is a charcoal burning stove and †'mbu' is a mosquito.

To An African Child

Some find summer's hard hot days
Its bright light lingering into night
too long. They long
for weather mild.

But winter's demands
for clothes, cover, hearth and heat
are much more wearying
to an African child.

MERRY

DAYENU (It Would Have Been Enough)

If it were only
bumping over dusty red, red roads
Dayenu

If it were only endless landscapes
melting into blue green haze
Dayenu

If it were only thatched mud huts
nestling gently in the sloping fields
Dayenu

If it were only those who are disabled
wanting me to stay and to talk
Dayenu

If it were only children's happy smiles
and gleeful waves
Dayenu

If it were only flat-top trees
against the blue, blue skies
Dayenu

If it were only the welcome I've received
in people's homes
Dayenu

If it were only dappled goats
nibbling at the jacaranda trees
Dayenu

My soul and I are reunited; at peace with one another

MERRY

Playfulness

Apricot Toast

Apricot toast! Apricot toast!
That is the breakfast
That you like the most.
And what is more
I've a sort of a hunch
That apricot chicken
Will do you for lunch.

Signed Monsterpotomous

PETER

Suarez Soaking

A massive thunder storm came and wen-ched
And we got dren -ched.

MERRY

Take Two

Take two twins
Two lovely children
Two to love
And laugh with.

Take to Guernsey
To holiday
To relax
And let off steam.

Take to golden beaches
To blue-green sea
To sculpture trails
To a soaking!

Take two children
Laughing together
Laughing with me.
Two for tea?

Two up?
Two –dle ooo?
Take two!
THANK YOU.

MERRY

24

Poor Potomous

As I was sitting in my chair
I felt a spider in my hair
I felt the wretched spider wriggle,
And even thought I heard it giggle!

And just when peace had come once more
Behind my chair a lion did roar!
Alone I was and full of fright
With not a single twin in sight.

An alligator seized my thumb
And a mosquito nipped my bum.
This potomous was really scared
Of these attacks when he was chaired.

A monster potomous sat on a wall
With such a big bang
It made all the bricks fall.
Down went the potomous
Bonk on the ground
And it scared all the people
That terrible sound!

Signed Pottymonsterous

PETER

For Emusement

We've got emus at the bottom of our garden,
They gobble apples that are lying on the ground.
They wear bow ties and pretty silk pyjamas,
But the tigers simply wouldn't stay around.

The emus haven't got a big computer
To calculate the size of bumblebees,
They fry their meals of hamburgers and earth-worms
And eat them as they lounge high in the trees.

Their games are rugby, blind man's buff and polo,
Ice-hockey helps them quickly to unwind.
Yet they hate the very sight of television
As they cannot have their morals undermined.

We've got emus at the bottom of our garden,
Doing research into how we humans act.
They rightly think we're absolutely crackers,
So they plan to emugrate. And that's a fact.

Dictated to **Peter Cross** by an elephant
on a trunk line.

Oh, Twins!

Oh, twins!
Quick, stand next to each other!
Put your faces together
Yeah, see your eyes are more this shape
And your cheeks more fat
I'm just pointing out the difference
Nothing wrong with that!

You're the one who's good at maths
So you must be good at English
And you must be the confident one, because you walk
more like this
So you must be the shy one
'Cause that's how it works, right?
Twins gotta be a binary
Left and dark, right and light

Oh! I just love twins!
I can tell the difference, see
By imposing my assumptions
On your young identities
Oh, twins
I've always wanted my own
We'd dress the same and play tricks on folks
I'd never be alone

Right, so you're the tomboy
So <u>you</u> must be the femme
'Cause you wear blue and you wear pink
So cute, just look at them!
Yes, I can tell the difference
Oh, what a piece of cake!
Your nose, your height, the way you speak
No need to double take

I can tell you two apart
It's so easy for me
I reduce you to one attribute
Squash your personality

When I've decided who you are
There's nothing you can do
See I've said you're the clever one
So that must be true
Which means the other isn't
'Cause you can't both be that
I don't see how that's hurtful
It's really just a fact!

What's it like being a twin?
Do you feel each other's pain?
Can you read each other's thoughts?
See into each other's brain?
Do you fancy the same people?
What on earth would you do?
Have you ever had a threesome?

Are you just the same person torn in two?

Why should I treat you like separate entities?
What's the difference really?
Aren't you just two sides of the same coin?
Aren't you just here to entertain me?

Oh, twins!

SUBIRA AND WANDIA

Uh Oh

Mama's started yelling
She is screaming out my name
What have I done THIS time?
It was Sasha lit the flame
And tried to set the dog on fire
It really was a game.

It was Sasha in the morning too
Who messed up all the books
So don't go blaming me again
And throwing dirty looks
Cos I only helped her reach them
I should be off the hook.

And who ate all the custard?
Not me, you must know that
I was waiting for my dinner.
Sasha gave it to the cat
I said she really shouldn't
Cos it makes the cat too fat.

Uh oh. Extra chores for me.
Who knew a glove puppet could get you
into so much trouble?

MERRY

30

Snapshots

Just an Ordinary Day

Just an ordinary day,
When Robert flew away.
Just a routine recce, flown at noon.
Robert, boxed by heavy flak,
Was three times hit. He came not back.

Just an ordinary loss,
When Robert hit the moss.
'One of many men died too soon ...
Tragic words, but commonplace,
Stupid; minding again his face.

Just an ordinary war,
With Mars and thundering Thor.
Death and Death across the earth and moon.
Comes another plane or gun
For Robert's ordinary son?

PETER

Pipe Smoke

Twirling, swirling, bluegrey curling,
Eddying up around my head;
Everchanging ghosts and phantoms
Briefly living – and are dead.
Born in fire; then upward wafting,
Slowly drifting to the sky.
Do they reach their own Valhalla,
Seen no more by human eye?
Are they merely like a thoughtflash,
Gone as quickly as they start?
Only this I know; these phantoms
Wraith contentment in my heart.

PETER

Images From An Autumn Garden

It is not a respectable, well groomed day;
the clouds, bedraggled,
have their hair anyhow,
blown about by irreverent wind.
The earth, damp leafed, heaves moisty sighs
into the chillively air.
Trills, cheeps and squawks
run headlong into each other,
in joyful birdsong chaos,
daring the eye to try to find the source.
Old leaves, rejected by the trees
in search of new life,
still proudly wear deep brown and orange
curling sensuously, inviting touch.
One blush pink stone sets itself
in emerald moss,
asking to be celebrated,
trying to set a better tone for the neighbourhood.
But already winter jasmine
splatters careless blobs of sunshine
amidst the misty grey.
In such a vibrant death
will spring be born.

MERRY

Night Light

Magical
Velvet blue midnight
Summernight
Warm scented blossom
Light, fluffy flowers
Pink and white.
Churches don't mean much to me,
but this one, this midsummer night
grew gently up,
light against, between,
white cherry trees and
softest sky.
Was mist adrift
Around the nearground
Or were my
Dreams floating there?
I don't mind,
My mind
Was happy.

MERRY

Acupuncture Treatment

Kind words..........

Lie down..........

Needles in..........

Yawns start..........

Tears trickle..........

Ears tickle..........

Needles out..........

Much later..........

Much less..........

PAIN   Thank you!

MERRY

Sculpture Trail

In leafy arches,
By bamboo curtains
Springing from the lakeside
Near softest paths
Sculpture surprises.

Ahead
A sleeping head
A glance, askance
An orange dance.

Poised in dappled light
Blazing openly
Springing brazenly
Nestling shyly
Balancing gracefully.

There to engage
There to challenge
There to puzzle
There to amuse
There to behold … Some, there to be sold

MERRY

In a Pandemic ... At Least

At least my garden seems spring-time normal
With trees budding and bees buzzing;
With songbirds serenading my soul.

At least my shadow seems sunshine normal
With a breeze bustling and brambles hustling;
With blossom promising me summer.

Nature looks after itself, one way or another.
We must learn from nature to look after each other.

MERRY

Messages

To Thine Own Self Be True

To thine own self be true
Whate'er the odds,
To thine own self be true
Honesty nods,
To thine own self be true
Dark though the way,
To thine own self be true
Thus always say.
To thine own self be true
Thus drink life's wine
And, though rewards be few,
Self respect thine!

PETER

On Your 14th Birthday, Maya

Beautiful girl.
You have entered
the mad, bad, world of politics
Calling out the ugliness
Whatever your private fears
And I am proud of you.

Beautiful girl.
Your work is getting harder
And you must ask 'What for'?
But grasp it firmly, sternly, for
Knowledge feeds your ability
To move forward with head held high.

Beautiful girl.
You have become a proud warrior
and I am proud to know you,
proud to be joined by you
in the struggle to end oppression,
proud to be your ungodlymother.

MERRY

I Can

So oft I've stood upon the brink
Disaster – black – beneath my feet.
So oft I've seen the smallest chink
Of light snuffed out. Darkness complete.

Each situation have I faced,
Met terror, yet have stood my ground.
My inner me I've not disgraced
For I have held! My courage found!

I cannot contemplate a fear
So strong that I can't stronger be;
For courage is the face I wear.
I know I can believe in me.

'I can' Because I say 'I will'!
I shall, because my heart is strong,
Achieve my goals, myself fulfil!
Be this my glory. This my song.

PETER

No Hurry

Dear love, enjoy each moment!
Make of time your friend
Savour all of living
For living is the end
To which you shape your purpose
To which your thoughts you bend
For which you give your loving.
To slow down is to mend.

Time and life your allies
For time there is to spare,
Treasure each occasion
Let living be your flair!
Life has much to offer
If totally aware,
If spending time is tending time
And taking time to care.

PETER

For Dad at 75

Three quarters of a century
through thick and thin you strode
always your own person
no matter what the load.

As a brave young airman, you
kept close to stars above,
fighting for your country,
holding out for love.

Married to a woman whose
great courage none can doubt
wedding troths made meaningful
by two who saw it out
most faithfully –
especially at the end
of Mummy's loving, fruitful life,
'tho both your hearts did rend.

Bringing up two daughters
we hope we've done you proud
chalk and cheese we may be
but we'd both say right out loud ...

Three quarters of a century
Congratulation's due
you're a father to be feted
SO HAPPY BIRTHDAY YOU!

MERRY

I Will Be Happy to Leave
(This Earth To You)

One plague seems to usher in more
Covid -19 arrived and opened a door to
Human locusts, stripping the shops;
Social Darwinism
letting the frail and old die first.

That's me.
Even if this virus fails to reach me;
I may shrivel from loneliness
Ache from lack of treatment
For these old joints of mine.

That is what I fear. Not death.
I have lived, loved and been loved.
Privileged, my friends hail from every continent.
My children are my heart's warmth.
Enough; I can go.

But beware.
The world will not be better
When those of us deemed unworthy
Are allowed to die.
Grief and shame will cover the land.

Yet we must always emerge
To remind you of the riches
We, who are weird and wonderful, offer.
The earth needs us as it needs all.
I will be happy to leave it to you.

MERRY

Comfort Your Hearts Dear Friends

Comfort your hearts, dear friends,
In these troubled times.
Revel in your memories of love,
of beauty, friendship and wonder.

I recall with greatest joy
My tumbling twins as little ones;
Climbing anything that challenged them,
Creators of endless smiles.

I recall with greatest joy
The sight and scent of frangipani;
Huge but perfect white and yellow blossoms
Fragrancing Mombasa's air.

I recall with greatest joy
Eager, upturned faces of children I taught;
Their cheek and laughter overlying
Truly kind and helpful hearts.

And I recall with greatest joy,
this song from Greenham Common days.
'You can forbid nearly everything
But you can't forbid me to think.
You can't forbid my tears to flow
and you can't stop my voice when I sing.

Comfort your hearts, dear friends,
In these troubled times.
Revel in your memories of love,
of beauty and wonder.

MERRY

Don't Touch My Hair

Don't touch my hair.
I know
You don't know any better
You think what's mine is yours to touch, grab, take,
consume

You forget
Your ancestors' blood-stained hands still grip my
ancestors' kingdoms
I remember
You remind me when you act like this
Casual entitlement seeping from the pores of your
unmelanated skin

You may want to adjust your behaviour, your colonial
inheritance is showing

When you shove your hands in my hair without asking
Or even ask but ignore my response
You show me exactly how much humanity you think I
have
How much respect you think I am due
For a moment, you treat me like the animal your
predecessors thought I was.
Pet my head like a dog that knows its place and won't
bite you

You violate my space, my body
In that age old tradition of your genealogy
And call it curiosity

My hair is not exotic
Is not unique
Is not different
To be explored, conquered or investigated
My hair is normal
Your people's beauty standards told me it wasn't
Forbade me to love myself
Told me I was ugly a thousand times until I believed it
Until I slathered burning poison over my curls until
they were fried into submission
'Til my hair broke and fell out and then you told me
again I was ugly

You are used to seeing black folks' hair hidden away
Approximations of hair that looks like yours masking
the beauty you shamed us into hiding
Now I have the audacity to no longer hide
To wear my curly crown with pride
So you have to take me down a notch
Remind me I am a curiosity at best
An attraction at a freak show due to my exotic features
Primitive at worst

Well the only primitive behaviour I see
Is when you echo our simian cousins
Reach out and grab what interests you
You may as well start flinging your own shit
No, you can't touch my fucking hair, you ain't got no
manners?

WANDIA

Rage and Resistance

My Background

My background is a huge white wall
A blank expanse
My background is a paleness where my brown looks black
My background is framed by blood red curtains
Tied in place around my stage
The spotlight is on me and
I
I
I
Freeze

You threw me on this stage, you
Grabbed me by the hips and flung me
You don't care that blue
Violet blooms on my skin
Bruises that don't stand out
Quite as much as I do
Here

You asked me where I'm from
No, where am I really from
My parents
And theirs
You don't give a shit that I grazed my knees being
shoved up here
Scarlet droplets
Strings of delicate hot beads
Appear as if by magic

A conjuring trick
(Applause, applause)
When you asked me
What my heritage is
Emergency red
You'd think you'd notice
But it doesn't stand out
Quite as much as I do
In front of this projector screen
Your fantasies beaming in white light upon it
You say
Black is the absence of colour, but I am so bright
You see absence
A black hole
In which you can stuff your racist childhood nursery
rhymes and minstrel cartoons
Your violent assumptions, your degradation
Your stereotypes and 'positive discrimination'
Your confusion, your distrust, your ignorance, your hate
I won't burst

But
If I did
You'd just see art
Splattered upon your milky canvas
Not pain
My frame
Is ivory
That's why you see me

What's my background, you ask?
It's a huge white wall   WANDIA

We Should Have Seen it Coming

Our governments have always been war-mongers
Happy to kill Others
So we should have seen it coming
The day this bloodlust would turn inwards
Turn to killing our own
Turn to contempt for us,
Its citizens and those who care for us.

Our governments have always pretended they
Were better than Others
So we should have seen it coming,
The day they'd be pretending to protect us
From the Covid killer
Despite the warnings loud and clear
By Other experts, round the globe

And on this day, when lives of doctors
Nurses, carers, seem to count for nothing
We should have seen it coming
That we disabled folk would fade from view
As councils drop us like hot coals
From Care Act duties
With Government permission.

So they've announced the
We Don't Care Act 2020; for disabled folk
No help with food, nor benefits raise;
No ventilator treatment despite need
No decency, just DNRs we're made to sign.
We should have seen it coming.

Maybe we did, maybe we did, I think WE did.

MERRY

Care

Care. Scraped out of society
Slowly, layer by layer
Like the resistant flesh of a gourd
By our 'true blue' British existence.
Care? Where?

Vicious benefit rules and sanctions
Fraudulent disability assessments
Bankrupt local councils
Broken NHS
Care? Where?

British society though, unheeding,
Is building a giant human scrap heap
We rot and burn, but rot spreads
As do our angry flames.
No care? Beware.

If you are lucky,
Your family cares
Or your partner cares
Or your friends care.
Keep them close.

MERRY

Villanelle: This Vast Entitled Bag of Air

This hopeless Boris has no care
With vanity so plain to see
His arrogance is now laid bare.

He loves himself, he loves his hair
Thinks not a jot of you or me
This hopeless Boris has no care

He bungles here, he mumbles there
Looks at his millions with great glee
His arrogance is now laid bare.

He's either holed up in his lair
Or lying by a glistening sea
This hopeless Boris has no care

Corona virus plans are – where?
Our questions make him turn and flee
His arrogance is now laid bare.

This vast entitled bag of air
Gesticulating wild and free
This hopeless Boris has no care
His arrogance is now laid bare.

MERRY

Cuddly Cummings

Cuddly Cummings clicked his pen
Clucking like a mother hen
Round his blond and fluffy chick,
Fearing he'd do something thick.

And Boris did.

Shaking hands with all he could
Bojo didn't feel so good
On the day the virus got him,
And the nurses' needles shot him.

So Cummings ran.

Briefings then by one and all
(Each one just before their fall
Into burning Covid's hands)
Took us to the Promised Lands.

More PPE!

The Promises came thick and fast
Masks and aprons, but aghast
Staff found only bin-bag cover
Who'd remain a Tory lover?

Too many.

'There'll be thousands right here soon',
Chanted Hancock, Bojo's goon
And they did in great big packs
Useless too, just plastic sacks.

What a waste!.

Far too many folk have cried,
NHS and care staff died.
Cummings and our PM too
Unkept Promises will rue.

They probably are, already.

MERRY

I'm Trying
(But so are the times)

I'm trying to stay positive
I'm trying not to sink
But with every social No Can Do
I'm nearer to the brink.

I'm trying to keep healthy
I'm trying to stay slim
But with more and more inactive days
The light of hope grows dim.

I'm trying not to hate the Toffs
I'm trying to be kind
But with every doc and nurse's death
It's further from my mind.

So damn you all who've made this worse
And damn the hate you spawn
My love's for those you trample on
Who need a brand new dawn.

We'll struggle on together now
Our wisdom, born of pain,
Will see us sweep your wealth aside
Make HUMANS great again!

MERRY

Coffee and Cream

This man said we look like coffee and cream
This man makes me wanna snatch up his eyes because
he's using them wrong
This man speaks with the confidence of someone who
can never really see another person, only what he wants
to see
This man thinks he's giving us a compliment
This man is wrong

I'm not coffee, but
If I was coffee, I'd be scalding hot, causing welts,
decimate your tastebuds, you tried too quick, you regret
it but it's too late coffee
If I was coffee, I'd be bitter, leaving a taste in the back of
your throat for too long, you're embarrassed to admit
but it makes you feel sick coffee
If I was coffee, I'd be stronger than you expected, gives
you the shakes, realise you can't handle it, makes you
shit yourself coffee

But I'm not coffee
I'm me
I'm a carnival of multiplicities within this skin that I
love so much
I'm a dancefloor for dualities twisting and writhing,
twerking and grinding beneath my surface
I'm a festival of complexities and contradictions,

identities and experiences barely contained by this
beautiful brown body
And this man had the audacity to tell me I look like
coffee

It's not the first, nor the last time I'll be compared to
something you'd like on your dinner table
Weak and childish racists who struggle to see people of
colour as real and whole
You like to fetishize and fantasize to try to make us
sweet and palatable
And I'm here to remind you that we're not

We're not coffee: mocha, mochachino, babychino, latte,
one of coffee two of cream, milky coffee, coffee bean
You can't buy us from your local Starbucks
We're not caramel: caramel wafers, caramel delight
You have no right
We're not chocolate: hot chocolate, chocolate milk,
oreo, nutella, bounty
We won't be sweet for you
We're not brown sugar, cinnamon, walnut, whisky
We're not here for your whimsy
We're not coconut, curry, little chili, hot sauce, sweet n
sour sauce
We will not spice up your life
We're not … mixed salad, olives and tahini, nandos
fucking chicken,
Fuck you though, dickhead ?!

We are more than you could ever consume
So don't you even think to presume
That this is anything more than
Objectifying,
fetishizing,
racist,
gross,
boring,
overplayed,
trashy garbage

(and no, it's not a fucking compliment)

SUBIRA

Reverse Racism and Other White Tears
(A Self-Care Guide For Black Kids Who Are Afraid Of White People)

Reverse racism
That's what they call it
When they stuck in their feelings about some
something or other
Someone called them Becky when their name is actually
Hannah
Someone told them their Post Malone cornrows got
them looking like a scarecrow

Someone told them that "actually, honey, you can't
twerk for shit"
Someone told them to take off that fancy dress shop
kimono
Someone snatched off their messy white girls night out
bindi
Someone called them crackers, caspers, Hellman's
mayosapiens, enemies of the sunlight, basic ass crusty
abominations, pasty white devils, dusty ass no lip havin
ass pale demons, nasty pink eared motherfuckers who
always gotta be making out with their dogs
Or not even
Or they went to a work meeting and someone raised
that they were making inappropriate jokes
Or someone asked "could you please stop touching my
hair?"

Or they saw a poster at the uni for a discussion group
that's only open to people of colour
Or they didn't understand the in-jokes on a facebook
thread that wasn't meant for them
Or a brown person more qualified than them got the
job or the uni place or the gig that they couldn't
Or someone called them out for tryna Rachel Dolezal
their way through the club
Or someone suggested the black person might know
more about black lives than they do

And they wanna cry and call it

Reverse racism

You see
When they do that
You can see clearly the whole shallow pool of their
understanding
They really think that racism is as basic as the
decorations on their Starbucks cup

That it's just being nasty
Being rude
Making kinda mean generalisations
(And honestly
If any of this being making you get in your feelings
Good)

I don't have time for white ignorance
The arrogance to overlook the structures that been
pointed, rigid and sharp at our necks from day
The structures built with the bodies of our ancestors for
the benefit of their ancestors
The structures that leave us little room to move, try to
restrict us from breathing, flourishing, thriving
I don't have the patience to sweetly explain
It's not like I haven't tried to before
But telling colonizers that we mad at them for
colonizing
Is not something that goes down well so often
And I'm not about to soften my approach any more
Because I already tried in my politest voice and that
didn't work
So I guess some people just gonna have to stay mad
Stay salty
Stay heated
Stay pressed
I'm not about to tone down this righteous black voice
So they can just go on and cry their silly white crocodile
tears
I'm not here for it
So Becky (Hannah)
Bye

SUBIRA

Clearing Out the Trash

Everybody's been hyping about this programme on
Netflix that teaches people how to tidy up
How to declutter your chaos
Say goodbye to the clothes that no longer serve you
Get rid of the 17 Tupperwares without lids, my god!
Storage solutions!
my girl teaches you how to fold
Marie Kondo says 'if it doesn't spark joy, you thank the
item and say goodbye'

Now I'm choosing to wildly misinterpret that
Or at least broaden it way out of its intended scope
Because there's a lot of things in the world that don't
bring me joy
and I'm about ready to take out the trash

To the white people who claim to be anti-racist just to
get points from their brown friends
Thank you
There were times it was genuinely great to have you here
But now you're hanging around awkwardly like a
jumper slipping off the hanger, shrunken and
misshapen by the wash
Looked okay to start with I guess
But on closer inspection there's stains of racism
Holes of cowardice
Loose threads unravelling how disingenuous a person
can be

It turns out a lot of white people will talk the anti racism
talk
But shrink like wool in a 60 wash when there's real life
racism in front of their very eyes
Always wanna make self deprecating 'white people'
jokes and set the world to rights over a pint
But when it's time to speak out it's as if their lips are
stitched shut like those jeans that tried their best to hold
my thighs but just weren't strong enough

You pretend to open up but the zipper is stuck
You pretend to be rock solid moral but I've seen you
warp like the plastic jug I left too close to the stove
You pretend to be supportive, but you're threadbare,
elastic stretched, sagging and useless
And whilst it can feel sad to let go and say goodbye to
something that's been in your life for some time
Sometimes there's nothing more beautiful than empty
shelves

I can fill them with something stronger, more reliable,
more me
Whatever I want and need
Because I've spent enough time hoping that my broken
things would somehow fix themselves
Hoping for my old jeans to somehow fit again
I've got a whole bag of clothes full of holes that I've
been planning to patch up
But they've been sat there a while now
And no amount of positive thinking is gonna sew them
back together

I've spent enough time hoping for you all to do better
Dropping hints that have scattered, unnoticed on the
floor like crumbs
Hoping that one of you will eventually pick them up
But it's all just gathering dust
Because at some point hope became about fingers
crossed complacency
But what change has crossing fingers ever brought us?
It was fingers gripping bricks, landing punches, fingers
making art, turning pages, fingers ripping up the
foundations of bigotry
Can't do any of that with fingers crossed
And I'm starting to think
That hope isn't enough

Thank you
I've learned a lot from you
But I'm growing and you're not prepared to grow too
I'm not going to keep squashing myself to fit your
narrow-minded views
And we all know if your wardrobe is full of too-tiny
throwbacks to when you used to be like that you don't
have no space to put the new you
It's time to take out the trash.

SUBIRA

Where Are You From?

Where are you from?
I'm from England
I'm from the UK
I'm from Great Britain, Rule Britannia
The great colonizers of the waves
I'm from a country whose wealth was created by slaves
A country built on thousands of Black and Brown
graves

Where are you from?
I'm from a small rainy island that still thinks itself
supreme
Nostalgic for our empire
So proud of our queen
I'm from a place whose violence radiates across the seas
Whose brutality grows deeper than the roots of great
oak trees

Where are you from?
I'm from a kingdom united in shame
A history profiting from Black and Brown pain
Salt on the sand, blood on the earth, displaced blame
Red splashed across the flag racists love to wave (whilst
calling immigrants a strain)

Where are you from?
I'm from a nation stained with atrocities
A place that I miss purely for the diversity
A land where I wasn't really a minority
Largely because of imperial history

Where are you from?
I'm from a country responsible for exportation
Of religion dealing in moral condemnation
That taught people to seek divine salvation
From problems that were always colonial creations

I'm from a really fucked up nation
A country that condemns others to damnation
Where its far beyond the collective imagination
To think that a brutal history of colonial exploitation
Might just be the reason for so much immigration

So you can see why we might be feeling frustration
'Cause it's difficult to answer with any elation
When people really want to know the location
Of what we're ashamed to call our home nation

WANDIA AND SUBIRA

CPSIA information can be obtained
at www.ICGtesting.com
Printed in the USA
LVHW012331030521
686351LV00006B/377